THE ENGLISH GENTLEMAN'S WIFE

THE ENGLISH GENTLEMAN'S WIFE

Douglas Sutherland

FOREWORD BY
DIANA, DUCHESS OF NEWCASTLE

INTRODUCTION BY
LADY WINDLESHAM (PRUDENCE GLYNN)

DRAWINGS BY
TIMOTHY JAQUES

THE VIKING PRESS

Published in 1979 by The Viking Press
625 Madison Avenue, New York, N.Y. 10022

Published simultaneously in Canada by
Penguin Books Canada Limited

Library of Congress catalog card number: 79-63198

ISBN 0-670-29680-5

Printed in Great Britain

Acknowledgements

I must confess that my publishers showed unusual perception in providing me with an editor with three undeniable virtues. Firstly she was female, secondly she was a lady, and thirdly she was a funny lady. Without Carol Illingworth's help disaster loomed.

I would also like to thank my sister-in-law, Annette Sutherland, who in addition to typing much of the manuscript can also spell, and my wife Diana for much material in spite of the fact that she denies hotly being a lady on the grounds that she is not married to a gentleman.

Produced by Gulliver Press Ltd

FOR MY MOTHER

without whose existence, and my wife, without whose
persistence, this book could never have been written.

Contents

Introduction

BY DIANA, DUCHESS OF NEWCASTLE

WITH the evolution of the status of women might the standing of gentlemens' wives be in jeopardy?

In the past everyone knew what it meant to be married to a gentleman and the Don Juans of those days kept their paramours in St. John's Wood or other places which varied slightly according to taste, time and fashion. Perhaps with the exception of some wives, everyone knew where they stood as long as a given set of circumstances prevailed.

Although times have changed, the female animal has not changed so very much. It is the way they go about things that has changed and been adapted to suit present day conditions. There are people today who do not wish to be married at all. An idea quite unheard of not so long ago. Many women of all milieux have the status of 'common law' wife, feeling perhaps that they have more chance of maintaining their freedom than their counterparts bound by the marriage vows.

Due to the emancipation of women the latter day twentieth century suitor has a different sort of competition with which to contend. A great deal of ground must be covered if he ever hopes to catch up with the young lovelies who can be out of reach in no time, flying an aeroplane, sailing around the world, driving a London bus or even an underground train; all of which makes today's swans sound like Russians. Rest assured, however, there are plenty of models, secretaries and, yes, debutantes, for the less adventurous suitor.

And where does all this put the conventional English gentleman's wife? Exactly where she's always been – plus ç a change, plus ç a reste. Either supporting local charities usually associated with the country squirearchy or struggling with the herbaceous borders, while in the meantime she is probably aware that *he* is whiling away the afternoon in dalliance with his current inspiration!

Once upon a time, many years ago when I had a pack of hounds, I virtually had to resign the Mastership due to lack of a 'surrogate wife', as no one domestic servant today could ever be coerced into undertaking the duties expected of an English Gentleman's Wife. I needed a 'wife' to scrub the breeches, polish the boots, sew on the buttons, drive my daughters to school, answer the telephone, deal with the chicken claims, fetch the dead and rotting flesh for the kennels. Then, after all this, make herself charming to everyone at the meet and generally arrange a Master's social life. But at that time, good 'wives' seemed to be at a premium, and I couldn't get one for love or money, even when concealing the fact that I didn't propose giving much of either of those commodities to any prospective applicant.

So for a time I struggled on alone and scarcely a day passed that I didn't regret the absence of a 'little woman'. After all, she wouldn't have been expected to do more than most gentlemen's wives. I already had some amateur help in the stables and any wife worth her keep can drive a horsebox, if properly encouraged. What English wife today – gentleman's or otherwise – gets more than one day off a month?

Which brings me to the point that a wife is a marvellous thing, something no gentleman should be without for too long. Anybody seriously considering the matrimonial stakes and with an hour or two to spare, should slip the mind into neutral, put the feet up and thoroughly enjoy an instructive read.

Introduction

NOT LONG AGO I entertained a very famous pianist at home. Now, we do own a piano, a beautiful Blüthner, made in Leipsig, cased in gold mahogany and possessing a tone which makes even my performance of the *Songs Without Words* acceptable in a large room, particularly if the children are playing Saturday Night Fever at the same time on the gramophone. Pianos are dear to the heart of a lady, and a source of security to their gentlemen, who can sleep soundly in the knowledge that however thorny the marital path his spouse is unlikely to quit his house in the middle of the night because ladies, being inately thrifty, she is going to want to take the boudoir grand with her and they happen to be almost impossible to get out of the window.

My visitor was however a Steinway artist, and I happened to know that she hit the ivories at approximately the same speed that James Hunt goes round Monza (or wherever) and with about the same pressure as a stiletto heel worn by an ample matron who is cross about what the butcher has sent up gouges into your parquet. Add to this the fact that dear Blüthner had been shipped down from London by splendid Messrs Pickford (the lady's removal firm) in the pouring rain and then shrouded for three months in elderly blankets loaned by my Mother while splendid Mr Hunt (a lady's builder) hacked away at the dry rot, the wet rot, the rising damp and the falling arches, all of which are an intrinsic part of Cotswold houses (lady's houses that is) in an atmosphere reminiscent of the battle of Austerlitz and you will see the cause of my concern.

Naturally you would never ask a great artist to perform when he/she is on a private visit. To do so would be as vulgar as asking an eminent physician his views on your state of health when sitting next to him at dinner, or enquiring from a chic divorce lawyer in the same houseparty just what is the definition of adultery. Given time, the eminent physician may volunteer that you ought to give up gin (bad news) and the lawyer may let slip that your husband will get custody if he finds out (bad news, too). Given time, the great artist may wish to ripple off a few more difficult preludes. The lady therefore takes the precaution of having the instrument tuned, so that no-body is going to be embarassed by a macedoine of dust, kittens and bits of Lego flying out of the works at the first thunderous chords.

I have related this story at length because it happens to illustrate one of the criteria for ladylikeness spelled out by Douglas Sutherland in this delicious book.

It was not, said she hastily, that I feared that after perusing *The English Lady* I might find out that I was not one, but more that one does love to have one's innate predjudices and opinions confirmed by authority, rather like reading The Times. No, for I belong indeed to that class of English society which regards the ancient and fully documented, though mostly obscure, lineage of my father's West Country family as superior to a married 'title' which suggests nothing more than a clump of rhododendrons near Sunningdale. The name to be sure sits prettily enough on the tongue, but Douglas Sutherland has told us in a previous work that gentlemen simply do not live in Surrey. Ah, but I do have an escape clause. The original Lord Windlesham, a gentleman of the greatest charm and public spiritedness had the bad luck to be born in frogland, was indeed half French. We all know that the French are both more urban and urbane in their living habits. Grandpapa probably thought Windlesham as handy for the seats of power at Westminster and Windsor, and as calm and rurally pleasing as do modern day courtiers the Bois de Boulogne and other fashionable banlieux.

There are however, one or two counts upon which I am definitely not a lady. First of all, I work. If gentlemen do not work, at any rate for overt pecuniary reward, it follows that ladies most certainly do not do so. My pecuniary reward is only too overt. It arrives by way of a narrow slip of white paper giving me the payroll number xyzsdz19553. That is all I can bear to read, because once I catch sight of the swingeing taxes levied on my poor struggles I feel an ominous quickening of the breath and flushing of the cheek and I have to resort to a sustaining nip of The Famous Grouse, which, being even more highly taxed than I, I cannot possibly afford.

To be fair, I am the first and only lady in my family who has worked. There is a tale told of a great aunt who was a bookmaker, but I am unsure of the details. I hope it is true though, because it does seem to me to be an excellent profession for a lady, or indeed any female, particularly if married. Flexible hours, no need to turn up unless you want to, sociable company, a built in adventure playground for the children, and the opportunity to mingle with the best people. The only other comparable job is piano tuning, and I have often wondered why more ladies do not take that up.

The second area where I depart from ladylikeness is in the question of the education of our children. I suspect that many ladies are either bored by or frightened of their children and thus stuff them off to Nanny and then boarding school at the earliest possible time. I happen to find ours an unending source of surprise and delight, knowledge and wit, though I do wish that they would not practice handsprings on my bed when I am in it, nor pull the tail off my aged leopard rug during over dramatic renditions of Tarzan and the Deadly Monster. So I disapprove of boarding schools unless you live in the wilds of nowhere, which I realise is where many ladies do live. They should move during the period of their children's education and take the example of the distinguished peer who spent term-time not a stone's throw from St Paul's in order that his beautiful and talented daughters might be properly educated.

I have had three main ambitions in my mature life, none of them ladylike. The first is to write a really good piece for The Times, the second is to have shoulder length blonde hair, and the third is to be created a duchess in my own right. I'm still working at the first, and ladies do not work. I have achieved the second with the help of M. Wella, but ladies do not colour their hair (I notice a lot of gentlemen seem to approve, though) and the third looks like being very difficult. Where are you, Carolus Rex? Ladies can be made and not born... aspirants may start by reading Major Sutherland's prescription.

LADY WINDLESHAM (PRUDENCE GLYNN)

1

The Origin of the Species

Queen Victoria invented the English Lady.

JUST as Stephenson invented the steam engine and Arkwright the Spinning Jenny to keep pace with the demands of the Industrial Revolution, so Victoria invented the English Lady to supply a need created by the developing British Empire.

For anyone to suggest that the English Lady existed before Victoria became Queen Empress is to betray a disturbing ignorance of the role women had hitherto played in the history of our island race.

Who can envisage the English Lady, as the world understands the description today, during the Regency, when gentlemen, by and large, exhibited good taste in all things except their personal habits in general and their choice of mistresses in particular.

Victorian society was almost entirely matriarchal and would never have tolerated Mrs Jordan displaying her undoubted talents as an actress to audiences up and down the country at the same time as her varying degrees of pregnancy with one or other of the ten children she bore the Duke of Clarence before his accession to the throne as William IV. It was only after his enthronement that she was allowed to die in penury, whilst he made ludicrous efforts to find a wife and legitimise the succession.

Even less would Victorian morality have put up with Charles II, who celebrated the Restoration of the Monarchy by foisting on the established aristocracy a plurality of bastard sons whom he created Dukes (Buccleuch, Southampton and

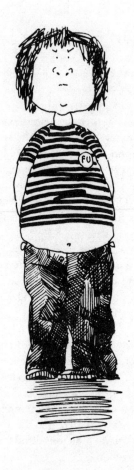

A boy for pleasure

Cleveland, Grafton, Northumberland, St Albans, and Richmond).

This is not to say that the role of women pre-Queen Victoria was unimportant. It should be noted that of our twenty-six surviving non-Royal Dukedoms only two were created for merit (Marlborough and Wellington), whilst almost all the rest owe their existence to the accretion of wealth by marrying heiresses or through Russian roulette in the Royal bedchamber.

All this, of course, lays great emphasis on the female. As has been recognised by perceptive heterosexuals since the beginning of time they have a vital role to play in the perpertuation of the human race. Even the old Eastern adage of 'a boy for pleasure and a goat for ecstasy' acknowledges as a first priority 'a woman for children'.

It would be tempting here to enter into a discussion of the differing attitudes to women in different civilisations, particularly the French, who surely most closely approximate to our own, or The United States of America, who equally surely must be the most derivative of both, but it is a temptation which must be resisted as not being within the scope of this work.

It is safe to say that throughout history the place of the gentleman of whatever nationality has carried with it, in the natural order of things, rights as well as obligations. By contrast, the traditional place of the woman has been to fulfil her obligations by producing children and keeping the house, in addition to making such financial contribution in the way of a dowry as she could afford. In return she had no rights at all.

It was only when the tiny determined figure of Queen Victoria seated herself firmly on the throne that 'a cloud no bigger than a man's hand' appeared on the horizon of the gentleman's understandable contentment with the *status quo*. Womankind may not have recognised the 21st June 1837 as an historic moment in their emancipation, but it was certainly to prove as important to them as the transportation of the Tolpuddle Martyrs was to prove to the Trade Union Movement.

Where four hundred years earlier John Knox had riled against 'the monstrous regiment of women', he was attacking the shadow rather than the reality. Perhaps even he realised this, when he took a teenage bride to his bosom as he tottered into crotchety old age. Of course, just as the peasants revolted from time to time against their lot, so women showed occasional flashes of spirit. Joan of Arc paid the penalty for meddling in men's affairs by being burnt at the stake for her temerity, and Mary Queen of Scots had her head cut off, not so much for what she did but for what she might have done.

By inventing the English Lady, however, Queen Victoria invented something tangible – a force to be reckoned with. She recognised the need for women to band together and abide by a strict set of rules which created at one and the same time their prison and their fortress. With the passing of the years some of the shackles fell away, but the entrenched position remained.

Today, when the supporters of Women's Lib seem to be hell bent on destroying their own defences, there are still some pockets of resistance where supporters of the concept of the English Lady not only stubbornly refuse to burn their bras but metaphorically draw the strings of their corsets even tighter. Before these heroic figures disappear forever from the scene, let us examine exactly what it means to be an English Lady.

To do this it is first necessary to recall the English Lady in her finest hour.

The Victorian Lady in the making

As has been remarked earlier, all women are born professionals. That is to say they are all born with a desire to achieve a good marriage, bear children, and live happily ever after. What young lady of whatever social grade does not yearn, from her earliest formative years, for the handsome prince in shining armour to carry her off on his white charger? The urge is, initially, not so much sexual as a desire to get away from her surroundings, whether they be a single-end tenement block or the rigours of a governess-controlled nursery in a castle.

Although the daydreams linger on, most sensible girls soon realise that knights in shining armour are in short supply and are ready to settle for the horse.

Boys go through a similarly romantic stage, seeing themselves in the role of St George who has to kill a ferocious dragon before he can win fair maid. These romanticisms are more practical, as any psychiatrist will explain. The ferocious dragon is, of course, the archetypal mother-in-law, whom he will have to overcome before he can get within a mashie shot of the fair maiden.

It was the method of going about the achievement of their ambition that characterised the Victorians. As their Commander-in-Chief, Queen Victoria's order of the day was 'reculez pour mieux sauter'. Overnight, bared bosoms disappeared from the front line of battle. Legs vanished behind a formidable fortification of innumerable petticoats and crinolines, from which 'her feet...like little mice, stole in and out, as if they feared the light'. In Ladies' drawing-rooms even the legs of the grand pianos were covered up lest they should excite unseemly passion in the breasts of the young men who came (by invitation) to pay their respects. Ladies attempted to demonstrate their purity by the whiteness of their skins, frequently washing is asses' milk or in the early morning dew and then spoiling the effect by superimposing a thick and often uneven coating of powder.

Until the time came for young girls to be launched, closely chaperoned, into Society they went through a process of brain-washing which would be frowned upon today in Lubianka Prison.

Few were sent to Boarding Schools, lest they came in contact with 'undesirable elements'. Education was by

'Her feet...like little mice'

governesses, who were for the most part frustrated spinsters and who inculcated such bromides as 'be good, sweet maid, and let who will be clever', which by any standards must be regarded as poor advice.

For the rest, they were put to regular Bible readings, petit-point and embroidery. They were also encouraged to sing and become proficient at the pianoforte. At the same time they were taught to think of the opposite sex as the enemy: libidinous, immoral, fortune-seeking, and unfaithful. If they referred to them at all, it was as if in inverted commas.

If this brief resume of the education of the embryo English Lady gives the impression that she was to be sent unarmed into the battle of the sexes, it would be completely wrong. The education of the young lady of quality had two purposes.

The first was, as in all competitive enterprises, to nobble the opposition. By using all the advantages of birth, her parents were able to give her a recognisable identity which would give an almost unassailable advantage over her less well-bred sisters. Secondly, she was being equipped against the day when she would be required to sally forth, grab the most prestigious husband she could and carry him back, as little damaged as possible, to his family home, which would then become her new fortress.

In order for this manoeuvre to succeed it must be remembered that at the same time all embryo gentlemen were being indoctrinated into the idea that it was their duty to marry a 'lady' – and if she should happen to be rich, so much the better.

D-day, if one may be excused for using a modern military expression, was the day when the groups of carefully trained young ladies debouched from the ramparts to be presented at Court. From the moment they had curtsied, white gloved, and with plumes nodding like Haute Ecole horses, to the Monarch, in theory at any rate, they broke out of the chrysalis stage and spread their wings, armed with a fierce determination to win. Their protective armour was an invincible belief that purity would prevail with a defensive weapon in reserve in the shape of a bottle of smelling salts, should they meet with adversity.

The formality of Court Presentations was really one of Queen Victoria's inventions. Prior to her accession, the aristocracy was a closely-knit group so small that everyone knew everyone else and there was no need for elaborate ceremonial and endless party-giving to enable their young to meet. Any of the aristocrats had the right to attend Court at any time they chose without prior invitation and this gave them the opportunity to introduce their offspring to the Monarch in the most informal way.

It was only with the coming of the Industrial Revolution that there emerged the new and socially ambitious rich who knew nobody of social standing. They were largely bankers and brewers, and indeed there were so many brewers that, on elevation to the almost inevitable Peerage, they became known as the Beerage. It was essential, in order to get their daughters presented at Court, to find a sponsor amongst the accepted aristocracy, which proved a profitable sideline amongst the more impecunious old dowagers, who charged through the nose for their patronage.

Queen Victoria found it amusing to lay down that these tottering old ruins should be encouraged by fashion to wear as low cut a dress as decency allowed, thus being forced to show the scrawniness of their ageing necks. The dowagers replied by wearing diamond chokers and parures so large that they concealed the ravages of time.

2

Schooldays and After

IT is now generally considered that young ladies whose mothers have social ambitions for them should be sent to a good school – 'good' generally being a synonym for expensive and preferably one where one or other of the Royal children are attending or have attended.

The practice of sending girls to boys' public schools, which have recently opened their doors to them to save their financial bacon, has not really caught on, although a few have appeared at Gordonstoun, presumably in the hope of catching a glimpse of Prince Andrew.

By and large girls' schools have retained their traditions of firm discipline and keep a sharp look out for any evidence of moral delinquency – good morals generally being considered more important than academic achievement. When the army took over occupation of Roedean, a very top person's girls' school, during the last war, the licentious soldiery were delighted to find above their dormitory bed spaces a notice which read: 'If you require a mistress during the night, please ring the bell'. Alas, the soldiers rang and rang in vain.

By and large, the age-old traditions are meticulously preserved. On a class outing the girls are still organised into 'crocodiles', with the littlest ones in front and the tallest ones behind, supervised by severe, shrill-voiced mistresses. On all occasions school uniform is *de rigeur,* although the colour grey is usually not favoured, perhaps because it is the colour most in use in Approved Schools for delinquents.

As in boys' schools, great emphasis is put on sport, the most upperclass team activity being lacrosse, a highly dangerous

A highly dangerous game

game, which results in a large number of young ladies having false front teeth fitted at an early age. It is also considered to be a great advantage to have a nearby riding school for all young ladies are expected to be proficient equestriennes.

It might be worth mentioning in this context a strange anomaly between upper class young ladies and those perhaps not so socially secure. Whilst the former, if asked, would claim 'riding' to be one of their interests the latter insist (vide any interviewee in a beauty competition) on describing their interest as '*horse* riding' presumably lest their judges should imagine that they had a preference for camels or elephants or whatever. I am not quite sure what this signifies.

At the same time, whilst nearby stables are considered desirable, to have a boys' school nearby is not; embryo ladies have to limit the first stirrings of sexual desire to senior girls or the games mistress.

On the whole many more girls are expelled from their schools for a variety of breaches of proper behaviour than boys are from theirs. In extreme cases despairing parents send them from expensive school to expensive school until they realise that they have a problem on their hands and finish up sending her to the local State school, where she has the time of her life. It was probably what she wanted in the first place.

The Coming Out:

The rules laid down by Queen Victoria lingered on long after her death. It was only after the last war, as the Empire started to disintegrate, that the scene started to change.

The real death blow came when our present Queen decided, with some justification, that the whole business of Court Presentation was time-wasting and boring that the rot set in in earnest – much to the relief, one suspects, of financially hard-pressed upper class fathers, who no longer had to feel guilty at not giving their daughters a proper start in life.

There were many rich and ruthless parents, however, who refused to bow to the wind of change. Aided and abetted by gossip columnists in the glossies, they determinedly continued to describe their daughters as Debutantes, having them curtsey to a large iced cake in Grosvenor House in lieu of the Monarch to mark the start of the Season. It was only a couple of years ago that the idiocy of this performance finally got through to even the most insensitive mothers.

It was only after the presentation had taken place that the young debutante was allowed, albeit heavily chaperoned, to mix with the opposite sex.

That embryo ladies were not the shrinking violets they liked to pretend is amply demonstrated by the vigour with which they conducted their marriage campaigns.

The first assault upon the enemy was rigorous indeed. Their male counterparts would have found involvement in the Crimean War, with all its hardships, preferable to what was entailed in young ladies 'doing the Season'. The mechanics of the whole business were time-consuming enough, entailing an endless round of dressmakers and milliners to be fitted in with regular attendance at one or other of the fashionable deportment schools where they learnt such basic skills as simple cookery and how to walk around balancing a book on their heads.

At the same time the social side was not limited to grand balls and other such stately occasions, but necessitated daily luncheon and tea parties, where debutantes and their mothers conspired together with other debutantes and their mothers to ensure that all the effort and expense would be worth while.

Should four months of the furious dancing far into the night, and the early morning appearances, immaculately attired astride a horse in Rotten Row, during four desperate months, not produce the desired result, it must not be thought that the young lady should then be allowed to return to her family home in the country and resign herself to marrying the local curate or take up breeding dogs. Far from it. A second campaign was immediately put into operation. This involved

...albeit heavily chaperoned.

the lady being sent to those parts of the British Empire where the presence of the army ensured a surfeit of sex-starved young men of good family, where it might be reasonably hoped that the heat of the sun and the shortage of competition might lead to securing the hand of at least a second son of good family and modest fortune.

Equipped with mosquito nets, solar topees, riding breeches, quinine and the inevitable bottles of sal volatile, they descended in droves on stations like Poona and Pondicherry. They were the front line troops of Queen Victoria's Own and the part they played in sustaining the morale of the Empire, as well as producing a whole new generation of Empire builders, should not be readily forgotten.

Now the captains and the kings have departed. The Empire on which the sun was supposed never to set is at one with the dust of Nineveh and Tyre. Yet there is evidence that the English Lady has not yet entirely disappeared, as I hope careful study of the following chapters will demonstrate.

Something so totally vulgar as 'doing the Season' is far too good an opportunity for the ostentatious to allow to be dropped altogether, and the nouveau riche still hire rooms in hotels and vie with each other on the number of bottles of champagne they can pour down the throats of a lot of rather rich but otherwise undistinguished young men. Indeed, if a young man of most modest means can get his name on 'the list', and plays his cards right, he can virtually eat and drink free for four months in the year, until the circus is abruptly terminated by the advent of the Goodwood Races, when Society migrates like a flock of starlings to Scotland for the grouse shooting.

It would be totally unfair to say that it is no longer the done thing to launch one's daughter into an increasingly commercial world. It is, however, generally considered by the less vulgar that a cocktail party, given in one's own home, or indeed for the well-to-do a private dance at their country house, is an adequate gesture before sending one's daughter to a suitable secretarial school in the hope that from then on she will be equipped to earn her own living.

The Lady in the Making:

Although the services of titled ladies are no longer in such demand to steer the newcomers through the social scene, there are still certain guidelines to help aspiring mothers in pointing their daughters in the correct direction.

One of these is 'the list', referred to above, which enjoys in social circles the same rating as a Top Secret document in the Ministry of Defence (or, possibly, the Ministry of Attack). Prepared by a lady columnist of great distinction and discretion, it is a list of all the eligible young males who, whether by virtue of good family or financial fortune, are considered suitable to ask to the round of parties which now constitute 'doing the Season'. Those who feature in this exclusive stud book are generally known as Deb's Delights or in the case of their more impecunious counterparts as male 'Sloane Rangers' from their practice of hanging around the various fashionable coffee-bars and pubs in close proximity to Sloane Square, in the hope of picking up nubile and financially eligible young ladies.

Unlike the Deb's Delights, the 'Sloane Rangers' are a much more irregular force, which includes many nattily dressed young men with carefully acquired upper class accents and a penchant for gate-crashing the smartest parties in search of a bride of sufficient means to ensure that they will not have to involve themselves in any distasteful commercial pursuits after he has married her.

Add to this the modern practice of the young of opposite sexes sharing flats and hunting in packs and it will be obvious that the task of the liberated young lady of identifying suitable husband material has become much more difficult. Queen Victoria would *not* have been amused.

Her back stiffens, her mouth snaps shut like a steel trap

3

The English Lady and her Wedding

THE English Lady, like her male counterpart, can be relied upon to preserve a stiff upper lip at all times of crisis, like having the elastic of her knickers snap in Fortnum & Mason's or being bucked off her hunter into the village duckpond.

The only exception to her determined composure is at the mention of weddings. Then her eyes go all misty, she clutches her bosom and the famous stiff upper lip trembles visibly for, to the Lady, as indeed to all females, romance is the very stuff of life. In this matter Kipling wrote truly when he said:

> 'The Colonel's Lady
> And Judy O'Grady
> Are sisters under the skin'.

Of course, it is a prerequisite to this reaction that the wedding should be a 'suitable' one. Should her daughter's inamorata not come up to mother's expectation, it is quite a different matter. Her back stiffens, her mouth snaps shut like a steel trap and her eyes sparkle like stars on a very frosty night indeed. A Lady whose daughter has become involved with someone with an unacceptable track record will refer to it as an 'infatuation'. Only if the prospective bridegroom comes up to snuff in all respects does she refer to it as love.

Assuming, however, that the match is approved, both mother and daughter, from the moment the announcement appears in *The Times*, enter into some sort of trance from which they only finally emerge when the bridal car sweeps away from the reception down the gravelled drive, with both of them in floods of tears. The husband, whose only role for months has been to supply a steady stream of cheques, will certainly not be in tears but almost equally certainly drunk.

The bridegroom-to-be has virtually nothing to do with the whole business. He is expected to call regularly, in case there are some orders he has to be given and to have his nomination of best man and ushers approved. In recognition of the monk-like conduct expected of him during the engagement period, he is permitted to get drunk with his closest friends on the night before the nuptials. His appearance the following day at St Margaret's, Westminster, with dark rings under his eyes, sheet-white face, and hands so shaky that he can scarcely get the wedding ring on the correct finger is charitably put down to deep emotion.

The attention to detail in the run-up period of a fashionable wedding is at least as great as one would expect of a General about to commit a whole army to battle. However friendly the bride's mother may have been with the bridegroom's parents, it all counts for nothing when the great operation gets under way. Indeed, they almost become the enemy, so desperate is she that any interference from them might mar her daughter's finest hour.

Whilst dress designers are driven frantic with orders and counter-orders about the getting together of the trousseau and sketches for the wedding dress are pored over and over again, there are a multitude of other matters of world-shaking importance which have to be personally attended to. Few mothers are content to hand over the catering entirely to one of the many highly qualified experts in the field, even the vicar is called in for a course on instruction on his duties, and a full scale rehearsal is carrried out to make sure that everyone understands what is expected of them on the BIG DAY.

All this activity is, however, dwarfed when it comes to drawing up the invitation list. It is on this ground that pitched battles are generally fought and a lady's commercial instincts blatantly revealed. She is torn between the need to ask the famous and titled, who are notoriously stingy in the presents

...charitably put down to deep emotion

they give but ensure a good showing in the Society magazines and the obvious advantages of asking the social climbing rich on the grounds that they can be relied upon to bear with them ostentatiously rich gifts. It is an opportunity, also, to pay off old scores by putting a blue pencil through the names of those who have for some reason offended in the past.

This latter practice can backfire. I recollect a lady of spirit who had been accorded the brush-off treatment and decided to get her own back. She wrote a polite refusal to the wedding to which she had not been asked on the grounds that she had a prior engagement and sent a richly wrapped parcel bearing the name of a top people's shop. When opened, it was found to contain a can of well-known deodorant.

On the great day itself ladies show a fierce determination that they shall reap every possible grain of credit from the occasion and take the greatest pride in everything going off without a hitch from the splendour of the flowers in the Church to the choice of hymns. It is, after all, their finest hour.

At the same time, it is to completely disregard the torment to which the guests are subjected.

It is bad enough that the men should be required to squeeze themselves into morning coats which no longer accommodate their expanding corporations or, alternatively, have been put to the considerable expense of hiring suitable attire from Moss Bros. Worse still is the dreadful ritual of the Reception.

No hostess in her right mind would insist under normal circumstances that her guests should be required to consume rich fruit cake accompanied by champagne, however excellent, at three o'clock in the afternoon. It is this appalling practice which leads many people to believe that champagne 'does not agree' with them. There is also the vulgar practice of displaying all the wedding gifts, so that the guests can sneer at the humbler offerings and criticise the over-expensive. And then, of course, to turn the final twist to the rack, there are the speeches. Speeches are a comparatively modern addition to the trials of attending a wedding. At the turn of the century before toasts were drunk speeches, especially long ones, were regarded as in bad taste. Whoever set about altering this admirable practice has much to answer for.

The only person who comes out of the whole business at all well is the bride's father who, if he is a wise man, will have a carefully concealed store of whisky with which he can anaesthetise himself and his intimate friends.

Weddings, popularly supposed to be the happiest day in a girl's life, in fact show off the English Lady at her worst.

4

The Lady at Home

BECAUSE of the changing habits of our present day young
ladies, the transition from her spinster days to becoming the
mistress of a gentleman's household is a decidedly more
traumatic experience than it would have been in a more
sedate age.

In the heyday of the English Lady it was merely a matter of
moving from one well-ordered household to another and her
main problems were not to upset the existing household staff
and to learn to live with the wallpaper which had originally
been chosen by her husband's grandmother.

Not so today. It is almost certain that the young lady, who
has achieved her ambition to marry a gentleman, will have
been to a good school and even had a spell at a finishing school
abroad – usually, for some reason, in Switzerland – but it is
equally certain that before the last mad dash to the altar she
will have been marking time in a state of almost indescribable
squalor in a flat in Kensington or Chelsea, or even Clapham or
Battersea, with an assortment of her contemporaries of both
sexes. She will intermittently have taken a number of
temporary jobs which she will find hard to reconcile with late
nights in fashionable 'in-places'. The resulting intervals of
unemployment will have been spent, for the most part, sitting
round in coffee houses, scarves knotted under chins, clutching
Gucci bags and discussing the relative merits of Philip or Rory.

For young ladies brought up in a gentlemanly household,
and for whom the interregnum of taking a bath in a forest of
dripping tights or searching for a clean cup in a kitchen piled
high with unwashed crockery has been comparatively short,

the transformation back to gracious living is not as difficult as for those of lesser social status who have been accustomed to life in a crowded flat all their lives.

Indeed, for the lady who has achieved promotion by marriage rather than been born to it, life can be very difficult. Her husband may treat her efforts to conform to the style of life expected of her with amused tolerance but, however much his friends' wives may protest their affection, she is only too aware that the slightest social gaffe will be the subject of much delighted comment behind her back.

Although a gentleman's house revolves around the master of the house, there are certain areas which are exclusively his wife's and it behoves her to assert her authority in these areas as quickly as possible.

If she is unlucky, she will find two main adversaries – the cook and the nannie, the latter having been isolated in 'Nannie's room' ever since the husband was first sent off to boarding school, but still a power to be reckoned with. Fortunately Cook and Nannie do not generally get on well together and, by exercise of considerable diplomacy, she will be able to play one off against the other.

In the case of the cook the kitchen is entirely her domain, but the lady of the house also has her own areas of jurisdiction. One of these is the still-room, for ladies take the greatest pride in making their own jam and bottling their own fruit from the walled garden. It is simply not done for a lady to buy a pot of jam at the grocer's and it is customary for ladies to compliment each other on their products, whether they consider them to be superior to their own or not.

A further traditional prerogative of the Lady is that she shall supervise the preparation of all puddings served in the dining room. She can, and generally does, consult with her cook on the daily menus, particularly if guests are expected, and for this purpose the cook is summoned at a certain time each morning and at the same time the gardener instructed what vegetables will be required. Thus, normally, the lady of the house never enters the kitchen except to ensure that such puddings as rice, semolina and a schoolboy favourite generally known as 'frogspawn' are served exactly as her husband has been accustomed to them all his life.

For a lady not to be able to make good milk puddings is, in the eyes of most gentlemen, sound grounds for a divorce.

If the lady's husband's house is particularly large, there are certain parts of it which she will seldom if ever visit. Reports that there is dry rot in the west wing leave her unmoved. As one lady remarked when informed on this point: 'Doesn't everybody have dry rot in the west wing?'

The centre of her existence, the flagship of her domain, as it were, is the drawing-room. It is a room which even her husband is wary about entering, except on large social occasions, preferring to lurk in the morning room, the gun room or the billiards room, according to the time of day.

So complete is her domination in the drawing-room that she may even be permitted to make daring alterations to the decor to the extent of having the curtains dyed a different colour or even moving the furniture round.

There are two things that can be counted on not to work in a lady's house. One is the table cigarette lighter in the drawing-room, and the other is clocks. This can be a disadvantage, as the lady never wears any form of personal watch. If she does, and inadvertently refers to it, it may embarrass her visitors who think they are staying too long.

Whilst, as has already been observed, a lady's day revolves around her husband's activities, like giving shooting parties and other equally time-consuming affairs, there is a part of the day which is hers and hers alone. This is tea time, which is taken in the drawing-room between the hours of half past three and five o'clock.

This is the time which is set aside for the entertainment of her friends or such necessary duties as having the vicar to tea or convening meetings to decide who shall undertake what duties at the forthcoming sale of work.

From the social aspect it should not be thought that tea time is purely an occasion for taking tea. It is very much more than that. It is an opportunity for the Lady of the House to demonstrate her most lady-like qualities to a highly discriminating audience. Many a lady's *savoir faire* has become suspect because the buttered toast was not considered to have been cut thinly enough (a sign of slackness below stairs) or because her tea service has not been demonstrably handed down from past generations. A newly bought service, however obviously expensive, just simply will not do.

The pitfalls into which the learner can fall are legion. Perhaps the most common is that she herself should put coals on the obligatory open fire without ringing for a maid, or preferably a butler, to perform the service. Equally, to serve cakes on those three-tiered cake-stands so beloved by the genteel seaside tea-rooms is regarded as quite outside the pale. They should be brought in with the muffins and buttered toast on the butler's tray.

Whilst a tea party, which is, of course, an exclusively female affair, can prove a nerve racking experience for the young bride, it can also be the highlight of the day for her guests for it provides an opportunity not only for inspecting the newcomer to their midst but is also an occasion for giving an airing to all those matters so dear to the female heart. The most popular subject is the shortcomings of those of their friends who do not happen to be present and criticism, given in the utmost confidence, of the perversity of their husbands in such matters as forgetting to apply for tickets to the Royal Enclosure at Ascot or to his propensity for spending too much time in his Club.

If an inexperienced young wife sometimes feels the strain of subjecting her domestic arrangements to the criticism of her friends, she can at least console herself with the knowledge that she is bound to be asked back for a return match in her friend's house, when the boot will be well and truly on the other foot.

A newly bought service, however obviously expensive,
just simply will not do.

Just as no man will admit to being a bad driver, no Lady will admit to being an inadequate hostess. Neither claim is true, alas.

An example of a thoughtful hostess (thoughtfulness being the essence of success) is that should she ask say a particularly distinguished musician amongst her guests she would under no circumstances embarrass him by asking him to play. On the other hand she would have seen that her piano was tuned to concert pitch just in case the great man decided of his own accord to perform.

The perceptive hostess goes to great lengths to ask people who will be witty and amusing to the other guests. On this account many homosexuals find themselves to be socially lionised because of their distinctive ability to amuse females who find them particularly sympathetic company.

Most ladies' husbands do not object to this. The fact that they themselves do not fraternise too closely is for no reason more personal than that they feel it might be catching – like chickenpox.

Foreigners also are regarded as quite a catch particularly if they can boast some sort of title however dubious, or have diplomatic status. By contrast those laying claim to a British title must be the genuine article for they can be quite sure that the less well-bred will scurry home immediately after the party and look them up in Debrett.

5

The Lady and Sex

ALTHOUGH in Victorian times sex was never very far from a lady's thoughts – indeed, it is difficult to imagine what else she had to think about – it was not an acceptable topic of conversation – and certainly not in mixed company.

The slightest hint of such matters and the lady would flutter her eyelids in confusion, blush behind her fan, and in extreme cases reach for her smelling salts.

It is an interesting social commentary that today fans have become collectors' items and a young assistant in a large chemist shop, when recently asked for smelling salts, looked puzzled and enquired if they were some sort of deodorant or for the bath.

This does not mean that the nature of women has changed since Eve appeared topless in the Garden of Eden. It is purely a matter of what women as a class consider to be the most effective attitude to take in achieving the designs they have on men.

Kipling, who showed an unlikely perception over the female of the species of whom, one has always rather suspected, he was slightly afraid, undoubtedly spoke the truth when he wrote so perceptively:

> 'When the Himalayan peasant meets the
> he-bear in his pride
> He shouts to scare the monster, who will often
> turn aside.
> But the she-bear thus accosted rends the
> peasant tooth and nail
> For the female of the species is more deadly
> than the male'.

...never very far from a lady's thoughts

It is quite understandable that Queen Victoria, contemplating the totally appalling immorality of her boorish Germanic forebears and their undignified scramble to discard their mistresses in order to sire a legitimate heir to the English throne, should have insisted on a greater degree of decorum amongst her courtiers, but there is no evidence that she herself was lacking in the amorous passions which had been characteristic of her ancestors.

Indeed, quite the contrary. The number of children she bore her Consort, her 'darling Bertie', does not suggest that she was solely concerned with her duty to provide a suitable heir to the throne. Her much quoted remark, 'We are not amused', does not reflect on her commonly assumed narrow-mindedness.

It was made on an occasion when one of her Guards' Regiments elected to play that estimable military march, 'Colonel Bogey', to which she could not possibly have taken exception, had she not known that the troops' version of the first line was 'Bollocks, was all the Band could play'. Few can doubt her very real attachment to her hairy Highland retainer, John Brown, which put even in its most innocent context must be taken as evidence that the passions she had inherited had not entirely died.

Certainly during the height of the Victorian era it was considered quite in order, after the fashion of the decadent French, for any man of social standing to keep a mistress whom, by tradition, he housed in comfortable circumstances in the then not-quite-so-fashionable area of St John's Wood. This was a situation which was generally accepted by wives, providing their husbands did not go on about it in front of their friends and were home in time to change for dinner.

By and large, Victorian ladies were divided into two categories – those who looked upon sex as a duty to accommodate a boorish husband whose wont it was to return to the matrimonial bed much the worse for a long session at the Club. Their classic advice to their daughters when the time came for them to be confronted with a similar situation was 'Lie back and think of the Empire'.

The other category was those who had the luck to capture a more romantic lover and who generally formed the opinion that sex was something 'far too good for the common people'. The result was that they saw to it that the servants' quarters of their houses were firmly barred – not as a precaution against burglary but to ensure that any female member of their large staff should be given as little opportunity as possible to escape for late night assignations and indulge herself of pleasures above her station after the housekeeper had locked the back door.

The fiction of upper-class Victorian morality is further given the lie by the popularity of houseparties, to which married couples of impeccable pedigree were asked and where the midnight traffic up and down the broad darkened corridors might be compared with Earls Court Underground in the present day during the rush hour. Today, of course, now that the ramparts of modesty have been thoroughly breached, there are few rules but one cannot help suspecting that the whole business has, in consequence, become much less fun.

It may be further observed that at this stage the sense of outrage which led to the banning of D. H. Lawrence's book, "Lady Chatterley's Lover", was largely because society ladies, safely married to dull husbands, felt that the book might be taken as seriously as Lawrence intended and their own delicious involvement with members of their husbands' outdoor staff (*never* indoor, unless with some particularly attractive footman) be subjected to a closer scrutiny. A friend puts forward the interesting theory about gamekeepers; is it because they are up and about at night?

Ladies and gentlemen, when married to one another, never touch or, worse still, hold hands in public. Communication at dinner with friends is likely to be limited, across the table, to questions such as: 'What's the name of the chap who fixed the piano after Hudson fell into it with the beer?' Even later in their lives together, they continue to sit at opposite ends of the dining table, communicating across the vasty wastes by ear trumpet.

The Gentleman never calls his wife by such pleasantries as 'sweetie'; he refers to her as 'dear old thing' (an expression of deep affection, and what he probably also calls his favourite dog or hunter). In moments of sarcasm, he may call her 'higher authority' or 'control'.

All of which is not to say that the English Lady may not enjoy a thoroughly satisfactory love life. It is only that she does not go on about it considering, with some justice, that such matters as whether or not her various animals are on heat or not to be a subject of much more general interest.

6

The Lady at Sport and Play

ENGLISH Ladies are not the helpless silly-little-me types who sit around, fluttering their eyelashes in the hope that some big, strong, and hopefully, handsome male will rush to their rescue.

Quite the contrary. English Ladies as a class are almost indecently energetic and competent. As the men are settling down for a quiet siesta after a good luncheon, it is always some Amazon who burst into the room crying: 'Who's for tennis?', or, no matter what the weather, gird themselves in an assortment of deerstalker hats, anoraks and wellies and drag everyone off on a five mile trek.

The result is that most Ladies, as the years advance, develop complexions of deep-sea fishermen, with a taste for the bottle.

The trouble, so far as men are concerned, is that ladies generally are frightfully *good at things*, and particularly at those things in which males take pride in excelling. Television viewers are inured to seeing ladies take the top honours, not only in the jumping arena but also in those fearsome cross-country events which require the maximum of stamina, whilst their prowess in the hunting field, even in the days when they were handicapped by having to ride side-saddle, is legendary.

If it stopped there, it might be acceptable to the chauvinistic male on the grounds that most young ladies spend their formative years almost entirely with, and in love with, horses but, unfortunately, this is far from being the case.

Ladies excel in such supposedly exclusively male sports as shooting, in spite of the fact that they generally shoot with a

Complexions of deep sea fishermen.

lighter gun than their male counterparts. This infuriates some husbands to such an extent that they try to bar their wives from their shooting parties, on the grounds that someone has to see to the supervision of the luncheon arrangements.

I can well remember a crisis in my own family when, after an all-male shooting party, the bag was laid out at the front door for inspection. It so happened that it had been a poor day, which led my mother to make some rather indiscreet remarks about the skill of the participants. 'Let me show you how it is done', she said, picking up a child's Diana air rifle which happened to be at hand. Putting it to her shoulder, she aimed at a bat fluttering high above her head in the gathering dusk, whilst the men smirked behind their hands. A moment later there was a scarcely audible 'phut' and the unfortunate pipistrelle collapsed in mid-flight.

It was the signal for the men to beat an undignified retreat to the gun room, where they stayed for a long time, fresh supplies of whisky being rushed in at regular intervals.

Fishing is another gentlemanly sport at which ladies have an aggravating habit of returning with the largest catches. The Queen Mother has a deservedly high reputation as a salmon fisherperson. Indeed, not only was the record for the heaviest salmon ever caught held by a lady friend of my family for many years but, when it was beaten, it was beaten by another lady. On the other hand, one cannot deny that there is an argument that ladies are born lucky. I can recollect one long cold day fishing for salmon on the Tay, both from the bank and a boat, which threatened to prove a blank, when at the last minute a large fish rose clean out of the water and landed back in the bottom of the boat – which was, of course, occupied by a lady!

Many and various are the excuses made by men for not playing mixed games with ladies. At tennis, for example, 'Much more fun for you girls to make up a four amongst yourselves. Make it less one-sided, you know'. Or, at croquet,

'Don't play with the ladies. Awful cheats, you know'.

There are certain games, however, where women are at a distinct disadvantage, not, let it be said, for lack of skill, but for inbuilt feminine characteristics. A typical example is bridge, where all but the most dedicated of women players cannot resist retailing the latest piece of gossip at great length in the middle of the bidding, which tends to destroy concentration, whilst at poker they have an aggravating habit of suddenly remarking, 'Does a flush beat a full house?', which has the effect of making her male opponents tear their hair with exasperation.

Machinery:

Another ladylike characteristic is a determination not to demonstrate their skill on any matter which they do not consider to fall within their proper province. Although they are adept at mending a complicated piece of machinery, like their electric sewing machine – and, indeed, would be horrified if any male member of the family were to lay a hand on it – they regard the motor car as an exclusively male preserve. Nevertheless, if put to it, they could show a much greater skill in, say, adjusting the points than their gentlemanly husbands who, as I have already remarked in my book on the habits of the English Gentleman, have absolutely no knowledge of what goes on under the bonnet.

(Incidentally, when discussing this curious reluctance of ladies to have anything to do with motor cars with a lady friend, she said: 'Stuff and nonsense! Whenever anything goes wrong with any of our family cars, we send for my grandmother!' This, I feel, must be the exception which proves the rule.)

This is not to say that ladies do not have an affection for their own cars, which they identify with even to the extent of always referring to it as 'she' and having a pet name for it, like a dog. They are, however, maddening as drivers, as any male

Does a flush beat a full house?

waiting patiently for a lady driver to vacate a parking space will confirm. By the time she has taken her seat behind the wheel, touched up her make-up in the driving-mirror, seen that her hat is set at the correct angle, and made a lengthy search in her handbag for the car keys, the man waiting for her to move out will either have burst a blood vessel or given the whole thing up as a bad job.

Whilst many ladies driving on their own can exhibit an expertness comparable with any man, if she is accompanied by a lady passenger, her driving is unpredictable to a point of being quite ridiculous. Whilst incessant chatter is quite harmless over the tea table, it can prove lethal when behind the wheel in heavy traffic.

Sometimes one feels that the determination of ladies is, to put it mildly, to be eccentric when it comes to motor cars. I will just quote one example which goes to show that I am not biased in this matter.

A middle-aged lady, who had recently learned to drive, conscientiously followed what she had been taught that, in starting her car when cold, she should pull out the choke. This she conscientiously did, and then would hang her handbag on it and motor around all day, with a cloud of blue smoke pouring out of her exhaust. This is why second-hand cars advertised as 'carefully driven by one lady owner' should be regarded with some suspicion.

Clubs:

In the last century ladies' clubs proliferated. The one difference between ladies' clubs and gentlemen's was that *no* gentlemen's club admitted ladies but *all* ladies' clubs admitted gentlemen. At some ladies' clubs even heavy gambling took place although most of them were innocent social meeting places. The last of the great ladies' clubs was the Ladies Curzon Club where before they were driven out by the gambling craze Dame Edith Sitwell used to entertain her friends daily to tea. Now the genteel clatter of tea cups has given way to the raucous cries of croupiers.

7

The Lady and her Money

Ladies are very careful with their money.

As someone once remarked, 'You can never satisfy a woman who has been accustomed to nothing' – a truth which many a gentleman who has married beneath him has discovered to his cost.

Those who are born into stately homes, however, have the principles of thrift firmly impressed upon them from their earliest years. Woe betide the embryo lady caught squeezing the toothpaste tube in the middle or going to sleep with the light on.

Ladies find the profligate ways of the lower classes quite shocking. I can still see the look of horrified amazement on the face of an extremely well-off lady describing how she had been visiting one of her husband's tenant's wives, when a parcel had arrived by post. 'Do you know', said the lady incredulously, '*She actually cut the string*'.

To cut the string of a parcel, however complicated the knot or however smothered in sealing wax, is something a lady would not do on any account, anxious though she might be to discover the contents. Up until not so long ago ladies were able to buy an ingenious little instrument to help them unpick particularly knotty knots, but there were some who regarded this as a form of cheating, rather like looking up the answers at the end of a crossword puzzle book.

When the knot has been finally triumphantly unravelled, it is wound up into a little ball and stored, together with countless other little balls of string, in a special box kept for the purpose. At the same time the wrapping paper is smoothed out, carefully folded and put away against the day when it will come in useful. As ladies usually have their parcels sent by the shop from which she has purchased her presents, the result is, with the passing of the years, that to open a cupboard door in a lady's house is to be inundated with a veritable avalanche of brown paper.

Another economy practised by all ladies is that they always mend their own underwear. I am really at a loss to know why this should be so, unless a lady's underwear has some deepseated connotations which a mere male cannot fathom. Nor, in general, do ladies send their underwear to the laundry, but have it hand-washed at home, either by a trusted maid or even themselves. (I am reliably informed that one exception to this rule is Her Majesty, The Queen, who, in London has her smalls sent to a very smart establishment not a stone's throw from Buckingham Palace.)

Ladies are also great counters. They are constantly counting their sheets and pillowcases, lest some thief has stolen away with them in the night, and the best silver is such a constant worry to her that she frequently has it locked away in the bank.

Ladies not only do not overtip but get very angry with their husbands if they think they have left too much on the plate for the waiter. Admittedly this is a rare occurrence, as gentlemen are also generally of the opinion that overtipping is ostentatious. Just the same, I have several times seen a lady remove a few coins from her husband's offering, when his attention is engaged elsewhere. Let it be said that this is not for her own enrichment, but simply because she is deeply imbued with a sense of thrift.

To say that a lady is by nature careful with her money is not in any way to say that she is mean. Whilst carefully sticking two wafer-thin pieces of soap together to make them last a bit longer, she is at the same time capable of acts of great generosity. Near relations are often the recipients of quite

...but get very angry with their husbands

valuable pieces of jewellery which she has grown tired of and she is good at remembering birthdays, when she will give quite unexpectedly expensive gifts, even to mere acquaintances.

The lady's attitude to jewellery is ambivalent. Most ladies would not thank their husbands for an extravagant gift of modern jewellery which is just as well as she is unlikely to get the opportunity, gentlemen not being much given to this sort of thing. On the other hand family heirlooms are treasured of to an extent far from justified by their real value. Ladies are seen at their worst when an aged relation dies without specifying what heirlooms are marked for whom. The in-fighting which follows such an omission is sometimes quite horrid to watch.

In the same way, when she goes shopping, she only buys things of the best quality, particularly handbags, shoes, gloves, and hats, which she has sent and which are sharply sent back again if on closer inspection they do not come up to expectations. She never goes to sales in smart stores and will not buy anything which has been reduced in price in the belief that there must be something wrong with it.

In view of the foregoing, it is curious to remark that most ladies have a passion for the humble 'Bring and Buy' sales, which are held constantly in order to keep the roof on the local parish church. They not only play a prominent part in organising them, and usually grab the prize job of running the White Elephant stall for themselves, but seldom come away without the back of the car being stuffed with everything from cracked plates to gramophones with the winding handle missing. These she then happily donates to the next 'Bring and Buy' sale, wondering how on earth she came into possession of them in the first place.

Ladies do not talk about money even to their closest friends. That is not to say that it is not done to complain about, for example, the increase in the price of hay to feed their horses; it is only the state of the family finances which is taboo as a subject because to complain about being very poor or boast about being very rich can only cause either embarrassment or boredom to their friends.

Nor is it really done to haggle about prices. As Oscar Wilde put it, 'a snob is someone who knows the price of everything and the value of nothing'. By this definition ladies are definitely not snobs.

I once sat next to a person at dinner who would most certainly have described herself as a lady but who had evidently not read Wilde. Practically every remark she made designed to impress the rest of the guests with her affluence. She met her match, however, when she turned to a distinguished portrait painter who was also a guest and demanded how much he would charge her for a full length portrait. The exasperated painter mentioned a sum which would even have shaken Jackie Onassis. Recovering her breath, the lady then asked how much a half length portrait would cost. "It depends which half", said the painter sweetly, whilst all the other guests gave him a silent cheer.

Ladies, however practical, can have peculiar ideas of rewards and prizes. At the Coronation of our present Majesty it was necessary, on account of the great number of Peeresses who were by right invited to the Coronation Ceremony, to erect an immensely dignified and comfortable convenience adjacent to the Abbey – a sort of aristocratic lean-to.

One of the first to use this was a well known Marchioness who unfortunately, on entering the plush lined box, had the misfortune to knock her tiara against the lintel, precipating it into the water closet.

Unable to retrieve it by her own efforts and unwilling to appear before her new Sovereign inadequately decorated she was lucky enough to enlist one of the Gold Staff Officers who managed to retrieve it with the use of his ceremonial sword. Being a Marchioness, unaccustomed to carry money, she rewarded her saviour with one of the Horlicks tablets with which she had equipped herself to sustain her throughout the long ceremonial which was to follow.

Where a lady is most generous of all is with her time. Few good causes appeal to her in vain, when it comes to a question of sitting on the committee or opening her gardens to the public, or raising money for starving races whose location she would be hard put to find on the map. Whilst her husband is spending a day at a shooting party, she is quite capable of spending hers presiding over a meeting in the village hall for the Prevention of Blood Sports or sitting on the committee charged with making arrangements for the next Hunt Ball.

Illogical the English Lady may be and thrifty to a point of eccentricity, but nobody would deny that she has a heart of gold, and where would all we lesser mortals be without her?

8
The Lady and her Children

The Nursery:

WHILST ladies readily perform their traditional role of producing children it is customary for them, as soon as they decently can after the umbilical cord has been severed, to see as little of them as possible.

This is not because their maternal instincts are any less strong than those further down the social scale but simply because they share with their husbands a belief that whilst any amateur can bear children, the problems of rearing them are best left to professionals.

In all gentlemen's homes, ample provision is made for nursery accommodation. There is a day nursery and a night nursery, and 'Nannie's Room' which, if she is a satisfactory nannie, becomes at one and the same time the refuge and confessional for not only the children, but quite often their father.

The most important figure in a young lady's early years is therefore her Nannie.

Nannies:

Nannies have long been recognised as a special breed. They occupy a position in a Lady's household which places them in terms of respectful intimacy with their mistress and quite firmly a cut above the other servants. This ambivalent position is particularly noticeable with regard to the next senior member of a lady's household who is by tradition the cook.

See as little of them as possible

Meals for Nanny and the children are always sent up to the nursery, which gives Nanny an unassailable advantage. To prove that she is a cut above Cook, she returns cottage pie to the kitchen with little notes like: 'You know Nannie does not like made up meat', the sort of thing which not unnaturally can drive a cook to a state of frustrated frenzy.

For Nannie, her little charges remain for ever small children. Second generation nannies can be quite appallingly rude and outspoken to the Mother and Father and even to grown-up children. Expect to hear such disconcerting remarks as: 'Nanny doesn't like the colour of those stockings, dear'; 'You know Nanny doesn't like you in that green shirt'; and 'Nanny thinks you are smoking too much'. These remarks are delivered with a hurt little sniff.

The lady's attitude to her children, particularly if they are girls, is one of reserved affection. They see to it that their creature-wants are readily supplied and they visit them several times a day. The most important time is after they have been bathed, powdered, eaten their evening gruel and, smelling sweetly of Johnson & Johnson's talcum powder, are comfortably tucked into their cots.

This ritual is as pleasing to the mother as it is to her children, who for the rest of their lives retain an indelible memory of a glamourous, evening-gowned Mummy, smelling deliciously of Chanel, as their last recollection of the day. Otherwise children are almost exclusively Nannie's responsibility. This is an arrangement which works extremely satisfactorily if the Nannie in question happens to be an old family retainer, who probably in her time had also nursed the mistress.

In my own case, my personal experience of Nannies was not a particularly happy one. Generally speaking, they were despotic, cantankerous or downright dangerous.

Lest the reader may think that the last description is setting the matter too highly, I would quote the case of one of my nannies whose duty it was to be at hand and cater for my

'Nanny thinks you are smoking too much'

childish needs whilst my parents were engaged in either giving, or attending, a dinner party.

As this particular nannie was conducting a vigorous lovelife of her own, she could not wait for my brother and me to fall asleep before she abandoned us for a more exciting evening.

In order to ensure that we would not waken prematurely in her absence, she took to the habit of turning on the gas fire in the night nursery and failing to light it. The result was, of course, that we very quickly fell into a very heavily drugged sleep, when she would turn it off and depart into the night.

It was only when my mother paid a surprise visit to the nursery after dinner, smoking, as was her custom, a small cheroot, that there was a blinding flash and she realised the full duplicity of our attendant.

Many other nannies came and went after a great deal of tears and heart searching, but this was the only one, as I recollect, who was shown the door the following morning.

It is only after her children have grown out of the swaddling clothes stage and can actually talk and walk, that the Lady begins to take a real interest in them.

It would of course be unthinkable that the girls in particular should not become proficient in handling their ponies, or that the boys should not be encouraged to mix with their social inferiors in the stable yard and gain a working knowledge of such important matters as ferreting for rabbits and shooting starlings with a .410.

All this is in the natural way of things, but of course there are many aspiring ladies who haven't quite made the grade who will use their daughters through the freemasonry of the local pony club to elevate their social status rather like theatrical Mums. Of course it does not always work out this way. Many a budding friendship has become frosted as a result of little Emily getting the winner's rosette which should, in the opinion of a rival mother, have gone to her Dolores.

Although ladies take a passing interest in the development of their progeny the policy of apartheid is continued, as soon as they have graduated from the nursery, by sending them to Boarding Schools on the grounds that it will help them to stand on their own feet in later life.

In earlier times this policy could be claimed to be reasonably successful as the boys could always be sent straight from school into the army or dispatched to administer the Colonies while the girls either got married or took up breeding dogs. Today things are not quite the same. When young Johnnie stops having his hair cut and goes off to live in a commune, and Felicity starts talking about taking trips and coming face to face with God, many parents puzzle about where they have gone wrong.

9

The Lady and her Garden

LADIES, by and large, are enthusiastic gardeners. Oscar Wilde had one of his female characters remarking acidly, 'Of course, my dear, I like to call a spade a spade', to which the other replied crushingly, 'Indeed! I do not recollect that I have ever seen a spade'. She was certainly no lady for it is very much part of being a lady to take an active interest in her garden, even if she limits her personal involvement only to picking the dead heads off the roses.

Many, however, are much more active, arming themselves with gardening gloves, skeps and trowels and priding themselves on their green fingers. Many, too, have a formidable grasp of not only the English, but the Latin names of all the flowers in her carefully tended herbaceous border — a talent which is seldom shared by her husband who is often hard pushed to distinguish a dandelion from a primrose.

The Lady's husband, although he is not allowed to interfere in the garden, is expected to do the unsporting things like spraying the greenfly and putting salt on the slugs. He also pays the gardener, and orders the manure. Manure is ticklish because it comes in different measurements all over the country. One lady I know of unwisely ordered two yards, thinking one yard sounded so little, and subsequently arrived home to find the house practically obscured by a veritable Mount Everest of best farmyard.

There is a further important aspect of a lady's gardening activities. Apart from the importance of being able to serve one's own vegetables and bottle one's own fruit, she takes great pride in being able to supply her own house and the church with flowers all the year round. Such is her pride in this achievement that she always arranges the flowers herself. When it comes to doing flowers in the church there is such competition amongst rival ladies that the vicar is forced to draw up a roster and woe betide him should it appear that one lady has been favoured above the others.

10

The Lady and the Church

LADIES go to church regularly and insist that their husbands and their children accompany them. They occupy the family pew, reserved for their exclusive use, with their house servants seated in the pew immediately behind. This does not mean to say that ladies are in general any more religious than the rest of us.

I can remember the case of the gentleman who had the right to appoint the vicar to the livings on his estate discussing the virtues of one of the incumbents with his wife. He gave it as his opinion that the incumbent in question was 'a dammed good chap', whilst his wife objected, on the rather original grounds that in her opinion the fellow was far too keen on religion.

The days when it was traditional to have family prayers, for which the whole household was democratically gathered together each morning in the servant's hall, is now almost entirely out of date, largely because servants are becoming extinct even more rapidly than their employers and anyway the servants' hall is now required as a children's rumpus room.

This makes putting on a proper show at church on Sundays all the more important. It is obligatory to wear a suitably striking hat and long gloves and smell slightly of camphor. No lady, incidentally, would ever be seen out with one of those neat little umbrellas so fashionable nowadays, which fold up in an incredibly small cover. A lady's umbrella is a formidable weapon usually with an ebony handle, which she uses to poke angily in the direction of those who offend her. The Lady, and the members of her family, each bring their own prayer book, it not being done to use the ones provided by the church.

She will have a good look round to see who else is there (and to compare other ladies' hats with her own), particularly her family's tenants and others, whom she feels should be following her example.

She and her husband disapprove of the so-called 'new' church services, and if the living is a private one, the Rector should watch out before he tries them on.

Bereft of his moment of glory when he read the family lessons at his own home, a lady's husband seeks compensation by reading the lessons in church with great gusto, particularly such passages as deal with fornication. He will read these from his own family bible, scornfully disregarding the one open ready on the lectern.

As for the children even a liberal supply of peppermint lumps does little to compensate them for dressing up for the occasion and quite often puts them off church until they get married and have children of their own whom they then subject to the same routine.

11

The Lady and her Wardrobe

Ladies do not overdress.

T H A T is not to say that they do not buy expensive clothes, but they certainly never indulge in the more extravagant sort of creations which one sees all the time in the fashionable glossies.

As most ladies spend most of their time in the country, they have a great number of tweedy things but on no account, tweedy things which they have bought in London. They buy tweed lengths from mills and have them made up by 'little women' which may not result in the elegance of their sisters of the trottoir but are just the thing for striding through the pheasant coverts.

Incidentally, all ladies have 'little women' to run things up for them and it is as bad form to poach another lady's little woman as it is to entice her servants away with the offer of higher wages. As mortal sins these make the pinching of her husband pale and venal by comparison.

Of course, when ladies first marry their gentlemen they do not immediately give up the vanities of their pre-marital days. Hermes head-scarves and other expensive items make their appearance at point-to-points and quite impractical shoes of great elegance. These conceits, however, gradually fade and the Lady soon begins to conform with all other ladies and dress like the Queen which is much the same as dressing like the Queen Mother. By and large they are at their best dressed for a brisk walk in the rain but they can look awe-inspiring at Hunt Balls and above all at weddings.

For men the black dress has overwhelming connotations

A must for every lady's wardrobe is that quintessential little black dress. People make jokes about it, and consider it old-fashioned, but this is neither true nor just. The little black dress, with Grannie's diamonds on the front and a string of good pearls, is elegant enough for a Royal Wedding. Black is flattering for all ages and sizes of women. Other ladies at parties, dressed in flamboyant bright coloured 'floaty' garments seem for some reason to be anathema to men (too overwhelming?). For men the black dress has deeply psychological connotations. From earliest childhood it represents the maid, or Cook, or Nannie, garnished as their sombre uniforms were with white pinnies, or the matriarchal widowed Grandmother. Later, there is the sympathetic waitress or barmaid at the local. Later still there is the elegant young woman, without apron, but still in the habit of sensible superiority, without looking vulgar. The wearer of the black dress at a party, be she pretty, elegant, shy, or ugly, will find herself with several men willing and eager to talk to her. Black may be a flattering colour, but there is more to the black dress than this; it represents security and authority in a manner not far removed from Grandmama's indulgence or Nannie's copious lap.

Foreigners who say that English Ladies are the worst dressed in the world are talking nonsense. Suppose for example all American women dressed like the wife of the President – or Dutch ladies like Queen Juliana – come to think of it, they do!

Here is a list of what you will find in a Lady's wardrobe:

Sheepskin coat, gloves and boots

About five pairs of wellies in various stages of decay

Long woolly knickers (which were part of her school uniform and which come from a top person's shop so last for ever)

Thick socks, probably hand-knitted by Nannie

Woolly gloves, ditto

Thick tweed skirts, and jerseys that nearly match

Cotton underclothes from Marks & Spencer

Matching dress and coat for summer weddings (like the Queen's)

Ditto wool for winter weddings (or if she is fortunate, a fur coat, for, as Nancy Mitford remarks, you never have to buy anything to wear underneath)

Cotton summer frocks in fabrics by either Liberty or Horrockses, made up by the little woman to a sort of shirt-waister design

Several pairs of thick trousers

One long-sleeved afternoon frock for opening bazaars

A selection of pairs of mocassin-type shoes from The London Shoe Company, called idlers, in assorted colours

Waterproof jerseys, jackets, hats.

Particular notice should be drawn to hats. Hats, for ladies, have a curiously uplifting quality. She has to have new ones frequently for such occasions as Ascot, Wimbledon, family weddings and the like; these can then be pensioned off for going to church in. Could it be that in a beautiful hat, and with the family jewels on, no one will notice what else the Lady wears?

However elderly and well-known the rest of her wardrobe, if the Lady is a horsewoman her riding clothes will be immaculate and in impeccable taste.

This is not to say that the articles will actually be in a wardrobe. All things useful are hung by the relevant doors, and most of the wellies are usually hors de combat because the farm cat has sneaked in and had kittens in them.

12

The Lady and her Relationships

Servants:

COMMENT from a Guernsey Charlady:

'A lady called when you was out – no I didn't come to 'er name – but I know she was a lady as she was covered with joolery and smelt of sherry.'

Nowadays, any lady is lucky if she can find someone to hoover the downstairs once a week, let alone clean the silver or take the dog or the children for walks. Living-in staff have become a thing of the past, and for better or worse ladies have to make do with a daily. These may charge a fortune, call their employer by her Christian name, come and go as they please, finish the gin, and treat the house like a hotel that doesn't charge for telephone calls. Ladies are generally fond of their dailies, and treat them as 'family'. As will be observed from the above quote, they don't miss much, and are therefore more valuable as confidantes than, say, Nannie.

As for gardeners, Ladies generally like their gardeners and the relationship is mutual. Gardeners are happiest in the greenhouse because it is warm, or talking about the relative merits of different breeds of bean. Like a good daily, a good gardener is regarded as a 'gem'. It is considered in appalling taste to try to pinch either from your friends. Very lucky ladies have a gardener who can actually double as a handyman, washing the cars and repairing the gutters. Because of their semi-indoor status these qualify, as does the daily, for cups of tea round the kitchen table, and a gossip. (The window cleaner also qualifies, and quite rightly so).

Because proper Nannies are becoming increasingly rare,

[63]

Ladies are often obliged to fall back on au pair girls. APG's are either a triumph or a disaster. The disasters are tiresome overweight foreigners, who cannot speak the language and are sullen to boot. They leave dripping tights in the bathroom, finish the gin, quarrel with the daily, and then get pregnant by the chap who drives the dog-meat van.

Shopkeepers:

Now the home farm has been sold to pay the death duties, and the moor is let to rich foreigners, ladies have to strike up a good relationship with the local shopkeepers. The butcher is probably the most important. Ladies are fussy about what they give their family and friends, and if there is no time to send the joint back they will go the next day and make a fuss. This is not to say that they will also thank the butcher roundly when the meat is good. This relationship means that with luck the butcher puts in scraps and delicious bones for the dog, and doesn't send best end of neck when you've ordered top side. Ladies like growing cabbages, and their families complain bitterly at eating greens for eight months of the year.

Hairdressers:

Ladies, particularly those who go regularly once or twice a week, have a relationship with their hairdresser. They always go to the same one, and, because by their nature hairdressers are sympathetic, they tell him ALL. The relationship with their doctor is different because the doctor has little or no time to listen to ALL, unless he is a psychiatrist, a breed that ladies tend to avoid. Even if they regard the doctor as a quack, the same does not go for the faith healer who cured the horse, or health farms, or the osteopath who unsticks bad backs. One does not talk about dentists.

Gamekeepers:

Ever since (and possibly before) D. H. Lawrence immortalised the gamekeeper, ladies have liked them a lot. Stories about gamekeepers are too numerous to recount here, but newspaper readers will recall that a titled lady actually ran away with hers last year. One suspects that she was only the tip of the iceberg. As a result, many gentlemen say that if they were not gentlemen, they would like to have been gamekeepers.

The Windowcleaner:

There is little to be said for window cleaners, except that they arrive at eight o'clock in the morning when you've been to a party the night before, and usually catch you in the bath. Window cleaners like a gossip and a cuppa, and why not? It is one of the most unfriendly jobs in the world, not counting the cold hands and freezing water; Ladies can do worse than confide in them.

The Lady and her dogs.

In general ladies prefer very small dogs perhaps on account of the fact that her husband is apt to have very large ones. They generally yap and snap at the slightest provocation but in the eyes of their mistress they can do no wrong. The lady's affection for her dog (and in severe cases a plurality of dogs) is in inverse proportion to her own love life. Fulfilled ladies take a rational attitude to their pets but the frustrated tend to lavish affection on the little brutes to a quite nauseating extent. They buy them jewel-encrusted collars, take them 'walkies' sitting on their laps in their motor cars, and cross off their visiting list anyone who does not send them birthday cards.

The result is that the animals, fed almost entirely on Fortnum and Mason bob-bons, become not only obese but tend to 'let-off' at frequent intervals. When this occurs the lady will look accusingly at the person who happens to be sitting nearest to her which causes the victim acute embarrassment.

Small dogs

Ladies who keep dogs as pets can be trying enough but when they take up breeding they are best given a wide berth. It is something which often happens to maiden ladies in middle age, rather like religion. Their highest ambition is to carry off the championship at somewhere like Crufts and there are no lengths to which they will not go to achieve this.

There was one very distinguished Peeress of the Realm who became infected with the dog breeding fever and by dint of the expenditure of vast sums of money eventually found herself leading her champion onto the platform to receive one of the highest accolades the doggy world has to offer. Unfortunately the beastly little animal snapped viciously at the judge as he bent to bestow a congratulatory pat – so viciously in fact that the little brute's false teeth flew out, resulting in its immediate disqualification.

Reminded daily how lucky she is

13

The Unmarried Lady

WHILST there are many non-Ladies who could only become Ladies by making a suitable marriage there are, of course, also quite a number of born-Ladies who do not make it to the altar.

Apart from sexual abnormality or more than ordinary plainness, the most usual reason for failure in the marriage stakes is that they come from families of high and even aristocratic status, but which are poverty stricken.

It is one of the traditions in families who have what are referred to as 'poor relations' – and there are few families, however grand, without them – that by and large they should not let the side down by taking the sort of job which could not be mentioned in the drawing-rooms of their richer cousins. Whereas the poor relation might have been perfectly happy working in a shoe shop or as a hairdresser's assistant, such careers are simply not open to them. In return the richer relations feel some sort of moral responsibility for their support.

Unfortunately this attitude is subject to a peculiar sort of double-think whereby the rich relation's conscience towards her poorer female relatives can be salved to her financial advantage.

It is these circumstances which has created that most tragic of all ladies, the Lady's 'companion'.

As most Ladies outlive their husbands by a considerable number of years they find it convenient to take under their patronage a lady who is preferably a relation in less favourable financial circumstances than themselves with whom she can converse as an equal and can accompany her on her annual sojourn to stay in one of those monstrous hotels filled with potted palms which line the south coast of England, and whom she can bully to her heart's content.

The Companion, long past the age when she could find other employment, finds herself hopelessly trapped and is reminded daily of how lucky she is. You can always tell the rich lady from her companion because her companion is the thin one who carries the suitcases and wears a rabbit skin collar.

14

The Lady and Divorce

THE English Lady by and large does not believe in divorce however difficult marriage may become.

In the event of it being forced upon her, however, it is back to the drawing board and she again assumes her professional status.

15

Ladies in Decline

ALTHOUGH there are still splendid English Ladies carrying on bravely in our rapidly changing society, there can be no doubt that their ranks are getting thinner.

It is hard to say at what point in history the impregnable position they enjoyed in the middle of the last century started to erode, but if I were to hazard a guess I would put it at the day that that pushy Lady Astor became the first lady to take a seat in the House of Commons. Although the only immediate and visible reaction in that hitherto entirely male preserve was for a sign to be erected outside their ablutions which declared it to be for 'Male Members Only', matters went far deeper than that. Today half the Cabinet may be female, even the Prime Minister, but between them they do not wield half the political power of the great political hostesses of the last century and the beginning of the 1900s. This may be a good thing from the mere male point of view, but is an example of the female of the species' determination to set a course of self-destruction. Lucretia Borgia did not serve the poisoned drink but it was her hand which mixed it, and the favourite wife of an Eastern Potentate was no less powerful for spending her life cut off from the outside world in a harem.

Lady Astor, by her ill-conceived action, did not strike a blow for her side in the battle of the sexes. Instead she inspired in a million female breasts the mistaken idea that they were downtrodden, misused, second class citizens.

In place of enjoying the comforts of their fortress homes the emancipated young ladies sought by every means in their power to break down the system which had so long protected

On the beach at Frinton

them. Squeaking excitedly about equal opportunities with men they battered at the imagined doors of male privilege from which many a male would gladly escape if he did not have a wife and children to support.

Of course the male 'privilege' of having to work for a living was only disputed by women in areas selected by themselves. Few insisted on being allowed to work at the coal face down a mine or go rat-catching in the sewers under London. Instead they clamoured for the equal right to be the 'chairperson' of I.C.I. or the Captainess of the Queen Elizabeth, or to appear on the beach at Frinton-on-Sea wearing only swimming trunks like the males they seem to envy.

The result of all this agitation has been of course obvious. Ungentlemanly males have started to insist, not without some justification, that females should also have the privilege of paying their share of romantic candlelit dinners and stolen kisses in the back of taxis. Quite suddenly it has seemed to be almost fuddy-duddy to bother to get married before setting up house and having children and who can blame the otherwise dull little couple living in a neat suburban two-up-and-two-down for imitating almost every goddess of stage, screen and radio who keep rabbitting on about 'love children' and referring to the once longed for marriage certificate as 'a useless piece of paper'. 'Our love is made in Heaven', they like to say before six weeks pass and the heavens appear to fall in and they part for ever.

'Not at all like the home life of our own dear Queen', as one very ladylike lady was heard to remark upon seeing Lady Macbeth on the stage for the first time.

And yet . . . and yet, somewhere in places like Throgmorton-in-the-Wold and Wittering-under Witchwood, there lurk the shades of the true English Ladies, once the most powerful influence in the greatest Empire the world has ever known. Long may they linger.

16

The Lady as Matriarch

THE English Lady only reaches her apotheosis in her later years. Elderly ladies are apt to soldier on long after they have buried their husbands. Thus released from the routine she has endured all her married life, she takes on a new lease and demonstrates characteristics which have lain dormant for many years.

To say that the matriarch is apt to become eccentric is perhaps putting it too strongly, but it is certain that she loses many of her inhibitions and becomes a colourful person.

It is still customary in many of the greater households when the eldest son inherits the Manor House that his widowed mother is expected to move into the Dower House, even if she has to be frog-marched there.

Dower Houses are, in fact, very often more comfortable and practical to run than the big house and it is from this point of vantage that the matriarch continues to rule the destinies of her family even more vigorously than when her husband was alive.

I remember a friend of mine describing a visit to a very matriarchal matriarch. She was shown into the drawing-room and invited to take a chair. Sitting rather nervously on the very edge of the nearest one she observed that the matriarch was gazing at her with what she took to be some animosity. 'Oh dear', said my friend, 'have I taken your chair?' 'They are *all* my chairs', snapped the old lady, leaving her visitor in greater confusion than ever.

One of the remaining delights of the elderly matriarch is 'putting people down' and they often go to quite elaborate lengths to contrive this situation. On occasions the conversation can become almost surrealist.

A passage of arms recently reported to me went something like this:

Matriarch to young married lady: 'Good afternoon, my dear. Do tell me, how are your two lovely children?'

'They are very well, thank you', said the polite but rather bewildered young mother.

'Don't be ridiculous', snapped the matriarch. 'You know perfectly well that you have only got one'.

It was nothing but the truth, and the victim's embarrassment can readily be imagined.

Another characteristic of the matriarch is playing a tantalising game with her nearest and dearest of 'Who gets What'.

Despite protests to the contrary, there are few relations who do not speculate what they might inherit. Many indeed show an ill-concealed impatience against the day when they can call the Chippendale chairs or the Gainsborough their own. This makes fertile ground for the matriarch. Her favourite opening gambit is to remark vaguely that she must make arrangements for her solicitor to come and see her about her Will. Having got her audience thoroughly tensed up and waiting to be told that the Gainsborough has indeed been earmarked for them, she will remark airily 'I think Cousin George should have all the family pictures. After all, I don't know where you would put them'. With acres of empty wall-space all the expectant heirs can do is clench their teeth and hope that nobody has noticed that their knuckles have gone white, for any protest would certainly ensure that their chances of inheritance would be very much less and perhaps disappear for ever.

As Grandmothers, Matriarchs can be a perfect nuisance. However strict they were with their own children, their grandchildren get impossibly spoilt. When they are little, Grandmama does destructive things like allowing (nay, encouraging) them to eat chocolates just before luncheon. As they grow up, Grandmama does even better. Expensive and unsuitable Christmas and birthday presents arrive; these are usually dangerous – motorbikes, .22 rifles, real archers' bows and arrows (with steel ends), and chemistry sets of the sort used by the IRA. She is also likely to take her grandchildren's side with a vengeance when they are expelled from their expensive school (she is not paying the fees) for setting the chapel on fire, thereby undermining the unfortunate parents' attempts at discipline for ever.

The Matriarch sits in the front pew at family weddings where, at the top of her voice, she tells dreadful true stories about either or both families. This not unnaturally upsets the Bride's mother, and if you are sitting further back you can see the feathers on her hat positively quivering with rage and emotion. If the Matriarch wishes to talk, everyone must listen.

In spite of these evidences of a sadistic nature, the Matriarch goes to considerable lengths to present the 'dear old lady' image to the world at large. On her infrequent trips to the village seated in the back of her elderly, but immaculately maintained, limousine, her progress is marked by the gracious raising of a gloved hand in greeting to anyone who looks in her direction, whether she knows them or not. She assumes, probably quite rightly, that they will certainly know her.

The same almost Royal dignity is maintained when condescending to pay a visit to a shop, and woe betide the shop-keeper who does not display just exactly the right degree of deference.

At the same time she shows a very real concern for the family tenants and their progeny. If she hears that any are ill – and she makes it her job to hear everything – she will arrive bearing sustaining gifts like calf's foot jelly and leave instructions that she is to be kept in close touch with the patient's progress. Most tenants' houses on big estates are full of pots of calf's foot jelly.

Christmas time in her old age recaptures some of the excitement of her girlhood. Endless lists are made out and suitable presents carefully chosen from the Army & Navy catalogue. She will take great delight in wrapping and labelling each present herself and summoning the family to a glass of sherry where their gifts will be distributed, whilst those destined for the lower orders are given to the vicar to distribute. Woe betide any recipient who does not write a thank you letter within forty-eight hours.

All in all, the Matriarch as an institution is almost essential to the proper conduct of the community over which she presides and her passing is the signal for a funeral which fills the parish church to overflowing, followed by a great deal of drunkenness in the village pub.